UNHEALED

Why Your Mental Health Will Never Be Healed In Hell?

MALIK J. AKBAR, MA, LMHC, LCPC

© 2025 Breaking BHAD Counseling, LLC

UNHEALED—
Why Your Mental Health Will Never Be Healed In Hell?

ISBN: 979-8-9994649-0-3

To request permission, contact Malik J. Akbar at mjakbar@breakingbhad.com or call 407.900.4825.

This book is dedicated to all who have escaped their internal hell, those who wish to escape their internal hell, and those who have no idea that they are in hell.

TABLE OF CONTENTS

INTRODUCTION:
No More Pretending

Stop pretending you're fine—especially when you're not!

I used to pretend that I was fine, too, but I eventually had to stop. I couldn't take it anymore. I had to escape hell at all costs.

Yes, I said it, "I had to escape hell." No, not the hell with black flames that are supposed to burn your self-regenerating skin while you scream and beg in unimaginable torment, drowning in fiery lakes of continual punishment. But I can't account for that, and so far, I don't know anyone who has been there.

As a fully grown adult, I must stay grounded in reality and true to my understanding of it. I don't conceptualize "hell" in the terms you may have heard or come to believe. But if you're looking for familiarity, be assured that the torment of "hell" as I've known it is equally filled with devils, demons, and other evil energies. They are just as monstrous, just as beastly, and just as ghoulish—but they're human.

In this hell, you come to realize there is an old, draconian system that holds power. They've managed to own and operate a corporate piece of real estate spanning 3,809,525 square miles of land for the past 249 years. It's a heaven for those whose privilege can persuade the unprivileged masses to vote against their own best interests. It's a heaven for those who convert political power into profit, as they inhumanely strip away the rights, liberty, and dignity of those deemed as "illegals."

As a Black man born and raised in the U.S.A., my family history stretches back a few generations. I can't say that I or any of my relatives have lived in a "heaven." I also don't know anyone from my old neighborhood who lived in such a "heaven."

To be completely transparent, the United States of America has been pure hell for me and millions of others who look like me, and surprisingly, for millions of others who don't look like me. This shared experience of suffering, often rooted in systemic inequalities, economic hardship, and social injustices, crosses racial and cultural lines, revealing a complex web of struggles that unite diverse communities in a collective yearning for real change and equity.

Every day of my life, I've been surrounded by a malevolent system filled with wicked people holding destructive ideologies who craft poisonous policies while pretending to be noble and caring. Once again, I must stay grounded in reality, so I accept that I can't fight these devils, demons, and other evil energies that exist around me in human form. To thrive, I had to ask myself in November 2023, "Malik, how can you escape hell?"

For weeks, months, and honestly, what feels like years, I asked myself this question—"how can I escape hell?" My dad and I would have long conversations during my early morning commute to work about society's theatrics, from politics to philosophy. Over time, I journaled my thoughts, conversations, and any feelings that arose in a series of notebooks. I hoped to someday piece them together—like now—and compile what I believed would best describe a metaphorical "hell."

While writing this book, I remembered something from my teenage years that has always stuck with me: I learned that "heaven and hell" are conditions of the mind. Later, I realized that this "condition of the mind" has been repeatedly expressed by scholars and philosophers throughout history. However, I firmly hold this idea because it's a fundamental truth, at least in my world.

From the mind, all things in existence are manifested. So, whether your mind is in "heaven" or "hell," you have a choice. At any time, you can change the direction of your life and influence those around you. Still, we all understand that no one's decision to choose one or the other is solely dependent on culture, ethnicity, or race. It includes everyone: men, women, and children.

Escaping from hell mentally and emotionally is difficult, but it's similar to escaping any other prison. In my view, breaking free from hell might even be easier than escaping a man-made prison. Still, escape is never simple because no wardens want prisoners to be free.

The word "escape" is an action verb, and like any action, that process begins inside oneself. The inner sanctuary of your mind might have once been a place of innocence, a metaphorical Garden of Eden where creativity knew no limits. Though it may seem childish, those thoughts and feelings once brought us joy.

If becoming an adult were the only reason for that joy disappearing, then how do we explain adults who write books and make movies for children? How do we explain adults who know how to go within the inner sanctuary of their thoughts and feelings to turn raw material into value? Doing so requires an escape within the mind.

Some escape through art, music, reading, meditation, exercise, and other healthy outlets. Others turn to drugs and alcohol to access that mental space. Yet, when major life events shake a person's thoughts and emotions, many adults are haunted by demons—whether present, past, or rooted in childhood. They see their lives as a battered and bruised body, scarred by life-changing events and circumstances they never faced, which become invisible scars.

If you're reading this, you probably know, or at least feel, that you must confront the hell inside you first. Doing so allows you to manage the hell that surrounds you. If you're truly one of "the chosen," you might even enjoy the rest of your time on Earth as an "Earthling," rather than a hellion.

Reversing decades of complex trauma, neglect, abuse, and negative self-talk cannot happen overnight. We also need to consider the many socio-political, economic, and cultural propaganda operations that occur daily in U.S. society. This work will require serious effort, organized planning, and a clear vision, along with a strong desire to evolve beyond the way we've lived for much of our lives.

You didn't get here by chance. You didn't pick up this book because life has been smooth and easy. You're here because something deep inside you is in chaos, and your spirit feels suffocated. Your spirit has been stitched together so many times that it's barely holding on.

You've been surviving, not truly healing, and there's a big difference—so don't let the world fool you into thinking otherwise. Survival wears the mask of healing. It shows up to work, smiles when needed, posts about boundaries, and schedules therapy— but beneath it all? The pain is still pounding.

The old wounds never entirely stopped bleeding. The patterns never shattered. The silence never truly ended. You've become skilled at pretending everything is fine.

You call it progress, but you're still stuck. You're still exhausted. You keep diminishing yourself just to fit in. You keep swallowing your pain under the false label of being "strong."

Acting as if you're healing isn't the same as truly living as if you're healing. Let's be brutally honest: you've been performing. You've been numbing yourself and calling it peace. Many of you have fooled yourselves for so long that each experience feels like a never-ending series of exhausting tasks.

You've been managing your trauma as if it's a job instead of facing it head-on. You tell yourselves that you're "growing," but in reality, you're just coping in more charming ways.

This isn't what healing looks like. Healing doesn't feel like self-betrayal. It doesn't leave you drained, disconnected, or disoriented. It doesn't keep you tied to places that poison your spirit just because they're familiar.

You cannot become whole in the same atmosphere that broke you. You cannot rise while still sleeping within the wound. This is part of the problem because, far too often, you believe that you'll make progress in the same place that pricks your skin every day.

The space matters. The people matter. The culture, the noise, the habits—they all matter. Healing is not only an internal process; it's also an external rebellion.

For those facing the external rebellion of it all, what if your peace feels like a performance? What happens when you silence your truth to "keep things cool"? I believe you know very well that's not healing.

If you can accept constructive criticism, then you should be able to understand that you're trapped by your own choices. You feel it—you've always felt it. I know that quiet ache in your gut every time you choose comfort over truth. There comes a time in your life when you grow tired of pretending to be okay, especially when you're barely holding on.

You've learned to keep the pain buried, to disguise it as control, perfectionism, people-pleasing, overworking, isolation, and rage. But buried pain doesn't die; it lies dormant, ready to influence, decide, and manifest in your relationships, choices, and voice—or your lack thereof.

And maybe, just maybe, the silence that once saved you is now the very thing that's killing you. It's sad, but you've been taught that healing must be painful, that it must break you before it builds you up. Guess what? We've all been taught that.

But a lie is created by systems that thrive on your brokenness. Healing isn't meant to keep you on your knees; it's intended to lift you to your feet, making you a force to be reckoned with against anything that ever tried to silence you.

Because here's the truth — they don't want you whole. The system's goal is to keep you "unhealed," stuck on the hamster wheel of burnout, anxiety, depression, and buried under a mountain of complex trauma that's older than you. It benefits from your disconnection, your dependence on external validation, and your inability to see your own worth.

Deep down, you know there's more. Don't you feel an inner power waiting to be reclaimed? A truth that, once uncovered, can shatter illusions of control and set you free from the cycle of stagnation. Only then can you begin to heal, rise, and reclaim the fullness of your life beyond the noise and limits of systems designed to keep you small.

A whole, healed version of you is powerful because it doesn't stay silent. A whole, healed version of you walks away, speaks up, and burns bridges that lead nowhere. A whole, healed version of you understands why you couldn't heal in hell — and it won't repeat that same lesson.

Let me be clear: this isn't a workbook. It's a warning shot. It's a manual for a mental and emotional jailbreak from the prison inside you — the hell within.

You don't need permission, so stop apologizing for wanting to be better (on your terms). Stop calling "survival," in and of itself, a success, and stop performing for systems that profit from your pain. At some point, life will require you to choose a path: either "false freedom" or "internalized liberation."

No matter what you choose, accept the cost that comes with it because freedom in hell is "NEVER" free. Everybody pays. And if you're not careful, you'll spend your life chasing permission, seeking approval, and going above and beyond under the illusion of mental health and well-being, pretending you're okay when you're not.

And speaking of cost, do you know what it will cost you? Without an itemized list of values to provide, here's what I can tell you. It costs comfort. It costs illusion…

It costs the version of you that made everyone else feel okay while you quietly unraveled. It costs relationships that depended on your silence, beliefs that held you back, and routines that kept you numb. It costs the dreams you once cherished, the passions that ignited your soul, and the sense of authenticity that makes you uniquely you. However, the most valuable thing it costs is the opportunity to live a life genuinely rooted in your truth and power.

That's the trade.
Wholeness for everything that isn't real.
Peace over performance.
Truth over tradition.

We're not going along with it anymore.
We're not waiting for approval.
We're not shrinking to fit into spaces that were never meant for us.

This time, we don't heal quietly. This time, we don't fold. This time, we rise—and if we have to burn the whole damn thing down to break free, then so be it.

Let's go away from being UNHEALED. Let's ESCAPE THE HELL INSIDE OF YOU.

Shots fired.

CHAPTER 1:
Understanding "Hell"—The Environment That Poisoned Your Mind

I magine trying to grow a garden in soil that is barren. No matter how much you water or nurture them, the plants struggle to thrive. Yet some of us still bloom—crooked, tired, but alive, not a failure, and that's resistance.

When you've had to bloom like that, pushing through concrete, growing sideways to reach a little light, it changes you. You learn to ration joy while learning to mistrust ease, and you adapt, but that adaptation comes with a cost. You end up confusing survival with strength and numbness with peace.

Welcome to hell! A world where your mental health is trapped in an environment that worsens it, rather than eases it. For many, that environment isn't just external—it's internalized, shaped by years of systemic oppression, trauma, and neglect.

And the worst part? You start to think the damage is your fault. That your struggle to feel okay is a personal failure, not a reflection of the conditions you've been trying to survive in. You internalize dysfunction as normal. You call it personality. You call it just how life is.

Hell, in this context, isn't a place of fiery torment but the oppressive, toxic spaces—whether emotional, social, or physical that undermine our capacity to heal. It's the persistent voice of doubt, the weight of generational pain, and the societal forces that tell us we're unworthy of peace.

Hell can be invisible because we're told it's normal: a 40-hour workweek that barely covers rent, a family that never discusses emotions, and a culture that applauds overachievers while overlooking the cost of burnout. You're not imagining the weight; it's simply that the world around you pretends it doesn't exist. Before we can begin to heal, we must first recognize these environments for what they are: barriers to liberation. We must also understand that true healing requires safe, nurturing spaces where growth is possible.

If growth and healing are your goals, then you must explore how external and internal hells—those harsh environments—shape our mental landscape and why escaping them is essential for effective healing. Healing in hell isn't noble; it's nearly impossible, like trying to water a plant in a drought. Effort alone can't outpace deprivation.

You start to question if you're just broken. You wonder why the tools aren't working. Why doesn't rest feel restful? Why does gratitude feel like a chore?

All this confusion is a byproduct of hell. This is what it does. It convinces you that your struggle to thrive in toxic conditions is a personal failing.

But let's be real clear: Hell doesn't always look like fire and brimstone. Sometimes, it appears as smiling faces in systems designed to break you: the school counselor who told you not to aim too high, the doctor who didn't believe your pain, or the workplace 'diversity' training that gaslights your reality. It sounds like "you're overreacting," "you just need to work harder," or my personal favorite: "Well, that's just the way things are."

But are you healing? It seems that you are standing in harm's way, waving your arms to let it know you're here. Meanwhile, you're still putting on a mask and seeking a thank-you from someone. If you're confused now, imagine how other parts of your life might be just as confusing.

It's not always the big traumas—it's the slow, constant drip. The coworker who constantly questions your tone. The therapist who doesn't get your context. The partner who says, "I didn't mean it like that," one too many times. It chips away at you. Death by a thousand cuts, but you're expected to smile through the bleeding.

We've been gaslit into thinking healing means being polite about our pain. Keep it quiet, keep it cute, keep it digestible. But when you've been raised in hell, surviving alone is already a rebellion. And if you've survived this far? You're already halfway to sacred.

Survival isn't passive. It's active. Every time you chose to stay, to show up, to care for someone else while your own heart was breaking—that was sacred. You weren't just coping. You were creating a life out of scraps. That's not weakness. That's alchemy.

This chapter isn't just about naming your environment—it's about reclaiming your *right* to call it what it truly is. You were never broken—you were *bent* by nonsense. There's a difference.

So when I say "you can't heal in hell," I'm not saying you can't heal *at all*. I'm saying you can't keep pretending the fire is holy and the smoke is air. The first step to real healing is stepping back enough to *see* that the place you've been told is home might be the battlefield where your spirit has been torn apart.

This may be the moment where you pause and think, '*Wait.*' *That's what I've been doing? That's what I've been calling normal?* And yeah, it might knock the wind out of you—but that clarity? That's the beginning of freedom.

And if that truth stings? Good. That's the wound finally waking up.

Healing requires air. And hell? Hell is airtight.

It's like trying to exhale in a locked room. No matter how hard you try to breathe, the air never feels clean. That's what it does to you—it keeps your body clenched, your mind racing, your spirit shrinking. And then it tells you to smile.

It suffocates truth, gags vulnerability, and turns survival into a performance—smiling big, nodding politely, being palatable while dying inside.

Now I know some of y'all reading this have been told that therapy is for "other people." Talking about your feelings is seen as a weakness. That naming your pain is considered a waste of time because "ain't nobody listening anyway." And I say this with love: *That's hell talking.* That's centuries of suppression whispering through your bloodline, hoping you'll stay silent and keep the system in place.

You're not just healing for yourself. You're breaking centuries of silence. You're unlearning what your parents were never taught,

14

ending cycles they saw as a means of survival. And that work? That's legacy work. That's real power.

But guess what? Your rage is justified. Your sadness is sacred. Your exhaustion is earned. You don't need to shrink to survive. You need to expand—and stop apologizing for the weight you carry.

Because here's the truth they don't print in textbooks: You are not crazy. You are reacting to an environment that was *never designed* for your joy. And no amount of mindfulness apps or "positive thinking" is gonna fix what's systemically trying to erase you.

This isn't about morning routines and green juice. This is about dismantling the systems that convinced you your anxiety was a personal flaw instead of a reaction to unrelenting stress caused by a political and socioeconomic system of psycho sociopathic politicians and wealth hoarders. It's not that healing tools don't help; it's that they weren't built to hold the full weight of oppression.

Healing starts when you stop gaslighting yourself. When you look around and admit out loud—*"This isn't me. This is the environment poisoning me."*

That awareness alone shifts everything. Because once you can name hell, you don't have to normalize it. You don't have to keep decorating it. You can finally begin the slow, necessary work of getting out of hell.

That's why we start here. With hell. With honesty. It's time to stop watering dead soil. It's time to find ground where healing can take root.

But before you find that ground, before healing can take root, you must radically accept a few things. You must accept that the soil you are watering can no longer be nourished as long as it's dead. You must accept that it will take several steps to rejuvenate that soil, and along with that acceptance, know that if patience and consistency aren't your strengths, then you're going to have your work cut out for you.

Rebuilding your inner soil and bringing it back to life will take time. So, ask yourself: Is it worth it? Will it improve the structure and restore the overall quality of life for all citizens who are willing to put in the effort to overcome the inner conflict created by a system that keeps us all in a state of perpetual turmoil?

What if the real revolution isn't out there in the streets, but in the moment you decide your suffering is no longer normal? When you refuse to let a system that feeds on your burnout, numbs your joy, and manipulates your pain dictate the pace or purpose of your life. Rebuilding your inner soil isn't just personal healing— it's political.

It's a direct threat to a machine that profits from your disconnection, despair, and silence. The moment you begin to nourish yourself, to center your well-being like it matters, you're reclaiming something they never wanted you to own: POWER.

The truth is, this system was never designed for your thriving. It was designed for your compliance. Your over-functioning. Your quiet suffering.

But healing—radical, intentional healing—is an act of collective rebellion. It says, "I refuse to be a cog. I refuse to be a casualty." And when enough people make that choice, when we stop mistaking endurance for empowerment and start rewriting what wellness means from the ground up, that's when the ground shifts. That's when we stop surviving and start rising.

So yeah, it's going to take time, and it's going to take discomfort—must I remind you that you're in hell? But what if the slow work of healing ourselves is also how we unearth a new future? One not built on extraction, oppression, or shame, but on rootedness, liberation, and joy that doesn't ask permission. That's not just recovery.

That's revolution.

CHAPTER 2:
The Roots of Trauma & Why Healing Is Difficult in Hellish, Toxic Environments

Let's stop pretending that trauma is simply what happened. Trauma is also what continues to happen when nothing changes. It's not just the blow — it's the bruise that never fades because life keeps pressing on it. In hell, this is just part of everyday life.

Trauma accumulates and worsens. It doesn't replace one event with another; it adds weight. A childhood wound becomes an adult trigger. A broken boundary turns into a belief that you're not worth protecting. Before you know it, you're carrying a lifetime of unresolved issues that all echo the same lie: "This is normal. This is fine. Keep going."

Many of us walk around with wounds so deep they've become part of our personality. We laugh to survive. We hustle to avoid pain. We disconnect so we don't fall apart. And people call it "resilience." No, that's trauma in disguise, baby. And it's exhausting.

What's tricky is that the world claps for trauma in disguise. They call you "strong" when you never ask for help. "Dependable" when you overextend yourself. "Positive" when you swallow your rage. And somewhere along the way, you start performing wellness because actual healing feels too unsafe to express.

What people miss is that trauma doesn't always scream. Sometimes, it performs. Sometimes, it overfunctions. Sometimes, it puts on a convincing smile so that even you forget you're hurting. And because the world rewards productivity, not pain, nobody ever questions the cost of your coping.

Burnout isn't just caused by overwork. It stems from feeling invisible in your struggles, from carrying heavy emotional burdens while others admire your grace. It's lonely. And the worst part? You might start to believe that if no one sees your pain, maybe it's not real.

Do you want to know why healing feels almost impossible? Because the very ground we're trying to stand on is still shaking. We're taught to meditate while still living with the abuser— whether that's a person, a policy, or a paycheck. How do you breathe deeply when every breath costs you your sanity?

And then they tell you to be grateful. To find the lesson. To trust the process. But how do you trust a process that's trying to erase you? How do you find "light and love" in a place that feeds on your silence? This isn't resistance, it's gaslighting with glitter on top.

How are you supposed to "do the work" when the workday itself is what's breaking you? How are you supposed to "hold space" when your own space feels like a trap? It's not a healing journey if you're walking through a minefield.

It's like being told to swim while someone keeps holding your head underwater. You're not learning how to float—you're learning how to hold your breath longer than anyone should have to. And in a world where Hell is the norm, most of the hellions would say that holding your breath longer than everyone else is the standard—but it's not.

Toxic spaces not only delay healing, but they also hinder it. They rewrite your DNA. They teach your nervous system to normalize the chaos.

They convince you that your pain is your personality, that hypervigilance is about being responsible, and that silence is strength. And after a while? You start mistaking survival for stability.

It shows up in subtle ways, like flinching when the phone rings or feeling guilty when you rest. Like that face you make to hide internal conflict and suppress genuine feelings, you know the one, right before you say, "I'm fine," because you don't know what else to say. You become fluent in the language of pretending —until pretending becomes who you think you are.

We adapt because we must. We shape ourselves into forms that don't even resemble us to get through the day. Then we wonder why we feel like strangers in our skin.

You end up losing track of who you were before the adaptations. Before the masks. You second-guess your voice. You abandon your own needs just to be easier to love, easier to manage, easier to keep around.

Let's call it what it is: Toxic environments are trauma factories. And no matter how many affirmations you tape to your mirror, if the space around you stays violent—physically, emotionally, spiritually—then your healing will always be in survival mode.

And here's the kicker: You can't self-care your way out of a system designed to crush you. You can't journal your way out of a job that devalues you. You can't sage the air and ignore the poison in the walls.

Healing can't just be individual work in a collective wound. You can do your breathwork and read all the books you like, but if the space you're in still shames honesty and punishes vulnerability, you're not healing—you're surviving with better language.

The worst part? Many of us have never experienced those environments. So we accept the trauma as normal. We treat dysfunction as part of the culture. We mistake endurance for empowerment. But trauma is not tradition. It's a wound passed down when healing was denied to the previous generation.

You're not only healing for yourself. You're rewriting the blueprint. You're breaking the silence that shaped you. You're providing your future self—and perhaps your future family—a map that doesn't begin with trauma and end in endurance. When no one discusses it, silence becomes a strategy. A survival mechanism. A way to belong in broken systems that punish honesty and reward quiet compliance.

But silence is not your story. You don't have to shrink just to be safe. You don't have to adapt just to be accepted. You get to be honest. Loud, messy, healing—and still worthy of love, even in progress.

I want you to understand that this is your reckoning. We're not here to be shamed, and neither are we here to cause shame. We aren't here to be anything like the people, places, and patterns that hijacked your healing and weaponized your silence. These are the forces that blamed you for bleeding when they handed you the knife.

We can't uproot pain unless we know where it's buried. So grab your metaphorical shovel. We're about to dig. Deep. Because healing doesn't begin with pretending things are okay. It starts with telling the truth about why they aren't. And that truth? It's not always polite. It's not always digestible.

Sometimes, the truth exposes the flaws in entire systems— family, education, economy, and cultural lies masked as patriotism or politeness. It reveals what has been hidden for generations, called "tradition," when it was trauma, and labeled "normal" when it was abuse. Healing involves bringing these buried roots into the light, even if it causes discomfort, especially if it does, because comfort has never been the foundation where justice grows.

You want to talk about healing? Let's discuss burning the scripts we were handed—the ones that told us to stay small, be grateful, obey, and suffer in silence. Let's talk about mourning not only what was done to us but also what we were never allowed to imagine because of it. Healing is rebellion against numbness. It's rage that refuses to be swallowed.

It's standing in the rubble of what broke you and saying, "Now I build." This work isn't just about personal peace—it's about collective liberation. Because when we heal in truth, we stop passing the wound down.

So dig deep, but dig loudly. Dig with anger and honesty. You don't dig because healing is cute, trendy, or something you can hashtag, but because you're done lying. You're done shrinking, and you're done decorating a prison cell and calling it home.

If you go deep enough, past the rot, past the shame, past the silence — you can't be controlled anymore because that's where freedom lives. Maybe, just maybe, you can start the process of escaping hell... Maybe.

Hell isn't just a place; it's a system, mindset, and design meant to keep you exhausted, distracted, and disconnected from your power. It's the internal voice that urges you to stay silent, the draining job, and the generational curse that no one talks about but everyone carries. Escaping hell isn't about fleeing; it's about awakening within it and realizing you don't belong there. It's about rejecting the roles they imposed on you: martyr, mule, machine.

The wildest part? When you start walking out—truly out—you begin to light the way for others. That terrifies those who would dare not challenge their outdated, inherited belief system. They understand the power of your healing, your liberation, and the movement it might become.

Remembering who you are means no going back, no shrinking, no apologizing, no asking permission to live authentically. Freedom doesn't come with fanfare; it comes with sweat, grief, and unlearning everything "they" taught you to survive but not to thrive. Once you touch your fire, the real work begins: building something holy in its place, something nobody can burn down.

CHAPTER 3:
Breaking Free: Recognizing the Chains That Hold You Back

Freedom can sometimes feel strange. We imagine it as a big, dramatic escape, like breaking out of a jail cell or quitting your job in a flashy way. But more often, it's about realizing you've been walking around with chains you didn't even notice. To avoid insulting anyone's intelligence, I'm sure you understand that they aren't on your wrists or ankles.

No—The chains you've been carrying are in your mind, in your habits, and in the way you talk to yourself. Of all things, the hardest truth to accept is that you created those chains yourself, link by link. Fear by fear. Rehearsed thought after rehearsed thought.

The real question is: can you see them? Can you identify them? Because that's the catch: you can't break what you *won't admit* exists. And you definitely can't change what you're still defending.

Many of us get stuck defending what hurts us just because it's familiar or because it worked once a long time ago, without stopping to ask if it still fits. Let's be honest: sometimes we don't even know where to start. Other times, we know *exactly* where to begin, and that's what scares us.

The truth is, not all prisons are made of bars. Some are built from stories—stories you've been repeating for so long they feel like facts. These facts have become the script that you and many others have followed for too long, and many have yet to realize they've been living in a simulation that was never meant for their growth, success, or peace of mind.

Stuff like, "I'm not good enough," "I always screw it up," and "People like me don't get that kind of life" don't shout. They whisper instead. These stories aren't loud; they're quiet.

They seem logical, realistic, and humble. While these stories sound true, they aren't the truth, but you think they are. They're chains disguised as common sense, and if you haven't noticed, not all sense is common.

That voice in your head telling you to play small? The one that says "maybe later," or "not for you," or "you're too much," or "you're not enough"? It's not protecting you; it's keeping you comfortable.

It wants you to be safe, predictable, and controllable. It fears change. It wants to keep you exactly where you are, even if that place is miserable.

Here's the question to ask: Where do these chains come from? Well, take a wild guess, because these chains come from many places—your childhood, culture, and family.

They come from that one teacher who humiliated you, maybe the ex who made you feel replaceable. Or maybe it was the time you were honest and got hurt for it. No matter where they come from, they've stayed with you for a long time.

Those moments taught you valuable lessons, some of which helped you survive at the time. So, you adapted, but in the process, you became quiet. You learned to stay small, agreeable, and safe.

But safety has made you too comfortable, removing you from the realization that you're no longer in survival mode. You're trying to grow a new set of skills—skills that will positively transform your life. This kind of growth requires different rules.

You can't run new software on outdated code. If you're still relying on software from twenty years ago, it's no wonder you feel stuck. It's no surprise you feel like you're glitching when life demands an upgrade. New software requires new code—and so do you.

Self-sabotage can be subtle because it doesn't always scream destruction. Sometimes, it appears as being busy, but it's just endlessly adjusting things or waiting for the perfect moment that never comes.

You don't apply. You don't ask. You don't post it, share it, or launch it. You convince yourself you're being smart—strategic, but deep down, you're just scared.

You're afraid of being seen. You're afraid of failing. You're afraid that if you expose yourself, it'll confirm your worst fear: *that you're not enough.*

And that fear? It feeds on your silence. It grows every time you step back. And then you sit in the dark, wondering why you feel stuck, when you've been dimming your own light all along.

So, how do you even start to untangle it? The first step is asking better questions. What do I tell myself when I try to step outside the box? Whose voice do I hear when I start to doubt? What am I avoiding, and what is that avoidance costing me? If fear wasn't in control, what would I do differently?

Write the answers down. Look for the patterns. They're there. You'll start to see where you're playing small and calling it wisdom.

Comfort zones can be deceptive. They appear safe, but they limit you. They trade your dreams for security, one small sacrifice at a time. You might think you're avoiding pain, but in reality, you're choosing regret.

Your brain favors what's predictable. But your future? That calls for a bit of chaos, risk, and boldness. Fear doesn't go away —you learn to move through it.

The good news is that these chains are made of thoughts and feelings, not steel and concrete. Although they seem real, like steel holding us tight, they are ultimately built from the stories we tell ourselves about who we are, what we deserve, and what is possible. These are stories, and stories can change.

Start small. Pick one belief that's been holding you back. Choose a thought that loops in your mind when you're feeling unsure, and ask yourself where it came from. Who told you that? Who benefits from you believing it? What evidence supports that it's even true?

Try something different, even if it feels awkward, and challenge those negative thoughts. Choose a different narrative, like "I'm learning," "I have something valuable to offer," or "It's safe to take up space." You don't have to believe the new story yet. But, be open to the possibility that maybe—just maybe—you've been wrong about yourself.

But what you don't realize is that this is how freedom begins: *with ownership.* And no, that doesn't mean ignoring the fact that your past didn't mess you up or that systems don't exist. Some of that stuff *is* real.

Ownership means asking, "Okay, now what? What can I do with what I've got?" Blame keeps you stuck, while ownership empowers you.

You didn't cause every wound. But healing? That's your journey to embrace.

Every day, you have a choice: do I keep repeating the old story, or do I write a new one? Writing a new story means saying "no" when you used to say "yes," and speaking up instead of swallowing it, while taking one step forward instead of spiraling into "what ifs." Action builds confidence, not the other way around.

The chains are invisible because they've been there for so long, and that's why you need people, not just yes-people. You need those who see your potential and won't let you settle—friends, therapists, coaches. These are the people who can help you recognize limitations you might not see and who believe in your potential until you start believing in it too. Sometimes, another person's faith in you is what breaks the chain.

If the map you've been following leads nowhere, maybe it's time to stop trying to adjust the route. Perhaps it's time to burn the whole damn map and start creating your own.

You get to do that. You're allowed. And you're more ready than you think.

Because who gave you that map in the first place? Who decided what your path should look like, and what success means? What does healing feel like? Who are you allowed to be?

Most of us receive blueprints built for survival within systems that never prioritize our freedom. We're told to follow paths paved with obedience, take detours filled with shame, and reach destinations that require sacrificing parts of ourselves. This is what hell offers: confusion, delusion, and illusion all wrapped up with decades of intergenerational trauma that you've compartmentalized throughout much of your life.

It's time to let that go. Let go of the idea that you have to earn your worth through suffering. Let go of the myth that there is only one "right" way to become whole.

Drawing your map means taking control of your life's story. It involves discarding the checklist that was never meant for your freedom and asking a deeper question: "What do I want to build that no one ever told me was possible?" That's where revolution starts—not in destroying everything out of anger, but in envisioning something bolder, freer, and more alive than anything before. You don't just rebuild; you reimagine and design the future from your own fire.

People might call you lost, reckless, or unrealistic—let them. Being lost could mean you are free from control. Reckless might indicate refusing to shrink back. Unrealistic could be exactly what this broken world needs.

You weren't meant to follow someone else's path. You were born to create your own. No matter what others say or think about you, that's the most radical thing you can do.

Carving your own path means refusing to be tamed by a system that thrives on your silence. It means saying no to the script, no to being the nice one, the quiet one, the one who keeps the peace while feeling torn inside. It's about choosing risk over routine, truth over tradition, and liberation over loyalty to systems that never truly cared for you.

It's the kind of rebellion that costs you comfort, but the payoff is something much greater: *yourself.* So, this isn't just about personal growth—it's about dismantling the lie that your life has to look like anyone else's to matter.

You're not here to blend in—you're here to *challenge the status quo.* To break the cycle of playing small. To be the first in your bloodline to declare, "This stops with me." Your courage to live fully, loudly, and unapologetically threatens every system built on your compliance.

Let it be—that's right, let it be. Allow your joy to be an act of defiance. Make your healing a middle finger to every system that tried to convince you that brokenness was your destiny.

Because the world doesn't change when people follow the rules; it changes when people decide those rules were never appropriate from the start. When you choose to live on your terms —trusting your instincts over their guidelines—you not only free yourself but also open the door for others to do the same. That's not selfish. That's legacy.

CHAPTER 4:
The Power of Safe Spaces While Building Healing Environments

You can't heal in chaos. That's just the truth. Growth doesn't happen when you're busy pretending everything's fine or putting on a show.

If we want to grow emotionally, spiritually, or in other ways, we need spaces that allow us to be our authentic selves. No masks. No need to pretend. Just genuine, raw, honest presence. In a complicated world like ours today, that kind of presence is quite rare. Because society trains us to perform. We are taught to smile for the camera, edit the caption, and show the highlight reel.

So, when you finally step into a space that doesn't require that from you, where no one's waiting for the perfect version, it can feel uncomfortable at first. Vulnerability always feels awkward before it becomes freeing. This isn't a sign that something is wrong; it shows that you're finally safe enough to lower the mask. Embrace that initial unease as the necessary bridge to genuine authenticity and deeper healing.

When I say "safe space," I don't just mean a cozy room or a quiet place. It's more than that. It's the energy in the air. The vibe. It's that feeling you get when you know you can be yourself without having to defend it, where your truth won't be twisted or tossed aside just because it makes someone uncomfortable.

Let me be clear: I don't mean comfort zones or echo chambers. I'm talking about places that welcome difficult conversations and deep emotions without shame. Places where you can be messy without feeling like a problem. The standard isn't perfection; it's being present.

Presence doesn't always mean knowing what to say or how to act. It simply means being *truly* present. Present with discomfort. Present with silence. Present with another person's truth without rushing to fix it or smooth it out. Safe spaces are created by people who know how to hold space, not dominate it.

The truth is that when people feel unsafe, judged, dismissed, or made to feel insignificant, they shut down. They hold back. They begin editing themselves, sometimes without even realizing it.

When this happens, healing is suppressed. Growth becomes silent, and we shift into a protective mode rather than an expansive one. Protection mode isn't just a mindset; it's a full-body response where shoulders lift, breaths become shallow, and the mind races.

You begin to anticipate rejection before it happens. You watch every word, gesture, and emotion, trying to feel secure, but it's not real safety. It's hypervigilance disguised as calm.

So, when is it safe for people to open up? When do real questions start getting asked, and honest answers begin to form? People stop pretending and start processing. That's where breakthroughs happen.

You can't grow when you're bracing for impact. You can't be vulnerable when you're busy armoring up. Healing requires a safe space—somewhere soft enough to lower your guard without fear of being hurt.

And here's the thing—safe spaces don't just appear out of nowhere. They need to be created intentionally, with care and consistency. You can build that kind of space for yourself. It starts from within. The way you talk to yourself influences how you expect others to treat you.

If your inner world feels hostile, even kindness can seem doubtful. That's why creating a safe space inside yourself is the first step. If you don't think you deserve gentleness, you will keep rejecting it when it appears.

Begin by examining how you speak to yourself. Are you compassionate or harsh? Can you be honest without criticizing yourself? It matters.

Speak to yourself as you would to someone you care about. Respect your needs, rest, set boundaries, nourish yourself, and cultivate joy; stop gaslighting your feelings. If it hurt, it hurt. You don't owe anyone an explanation for why something got under your skin.

You don't need to prove your pain to set boundaries. You don't have to walk people through your trauma history just to get permission to rest. If something feels wrong, that's enough. Respect that, and validate your own experience first, even if no one else understands it yet.

Then look outward. Who are you letting into your life? Who gets access to your energy? Who do you allow to speak into your world? Choose wisely. And when you do let people in, make your boundaries clear. Don't apologize for them. Boundaries teach others how to treat you, and they remind you how to treat yourself.

Boundaries aren't walls—they're filters. They allow in what nurtures you and block what drains you, and when you apply them consistently, something changes. You stop trying to be liked by everyone. You begin to focus on feeling safe with yourself.

Even the space around you matters. Your home, your room, and your work setup—all send signals to your nervous system. Light, sound, colors, clutter—all of these elements influence our state of mind more than we realize. Create an environment that promotes your peace, not your stress.

Your nervous system responds to various stimuli, including light, noise, temperature, and touch. If your space feels chaotic, your mind will mirror that. You don't have to fix your whole room overnight, but start with one corner.

One candle. One quiet space to land. Healing starts where you do.

Of course, this isn't just about you. Healing is personal, but it's also collective. There is something powerful about healing in community, and being around people who are on a similar path, even if their journeys differ. Being in spaces where truth is embraced, where no one's trying to fix, judge, or erase you, is sacred.

Whether it's a friend, a group, a therapist, or a creative space where people get honest with each other, that shared vulnerability creates momentum. One person shows up honestly, and suddenly others feel safe enough to do the same. Whether you agree or disagree, that's how healing spreads and how courage becomes contagious.

There's even a term for all this in the research world: psychological safety. It's not just some feel-good concept—it's studied, measured, and deeply tied to performance, well-being, and growth. It's the ability to speak up without fear of being punished or humiliated. And it doesn't mean we're all nice all the time. It means we trust that our voice won't be used against us. That's what makes it safe to risk being real.

That's why safety isn't about perfection—it's about trust. Can I show up as I am and not get punished for it? Can I speak from my pain and still be welcomed? That's what people are asking when they're checking if a space is safe, and that kind of trust can't be forced; it has to be earned.

There's a flip side to the situation as well. Unsafe spaces are easy to recognize once you know the signs: constant judgment, emotional dismissal, fake empathy that leads nowhere, a lack of boundaries, and toxic positivity that tells you to smile while you're falling apart. If a space makes you shrink or lie just to be accepted, it's not safe, and it's not where your healing belongs.

It's okay to walk away even if they're family. Even if they're friends, or you've invested years, you're not abandoning anyone. Choosing yourself isn't selfish; it's necessary. Some spaces only feel safe because you've gotten used to betraying yourself in them.

So, how do you become that safe space for someone else? Start by showing up, and when you do, don't listen to respond; instead, listen to understand. Let people feel what they feel without jumping in to fix it.

Respect their choices about what to share and keep their trust. Ask permission before giving advice, and if you make a bad choice, as everyone does, take responsibility. Intent is important, but the effect is more important.

Being a safe space doesn't mean never messing up. It means being accountable when you do. It means staying teachable. It means caring more about connection than being right. That kind of humility is healing in action.

Even the way we design our spaces influences healing. Architects and educators understand this. Trauma-informed design is a real concept that proves light and space matter. Think about colors, textures, and sounds—elements that also play a major role. We respond to our environment, and when it signals "you're safe," we naturally start to relax.

You don't need a design degree to create a healing space, but you do need intention. Ask yourself: Does this space calm me or stress me out? What needs to change for me to feel more at ease here? Start there. Your body will let you know what feels safe.

One more thing, it's crucial to realize that safe doesn't always mean comfortable. It doesn't mean easy, and sometimes the truth hurts. Sometimes growth feels like stretching a sore muscle, but safe spaces accept that discomfort because they trust the process. Safe spaces allow the tough stuff to happen without cruelty and shame.

Healing can sometimes cause pain, and that's part of the process, but it should never feel like *harm*. Pain may be part of the healing process, but cruelty is never necessary. When you don't know what healing looks like, it can trick you into thinking it's an act of cruelty.

Don't confuse growth with punishment or accountability with shame. Safe spaces make room for your complete healing process, even the messy, uncertain, or slow parts. It's not just about creating safe spaces; it's about being one. Let your presence be the permission someone needs to breathe easier.

To *be* honest and *feel* supported, you don't need to have all the answers. Just be the kind of person who makes others feel comfortable enough to show up unfiltered. This applies to everyone you meet and everywhere you go, as long as people feel like they can breathe easy.

In a world that constantly demands performance, perfection, politeness, and productivity, being a safe space is a radical act of resistance. It says: "You don't have to be impressive to be worthy." It says, "You can cry here, rage here, be unsure, undone, and still deserving of love."

This kind of presence disrupts every lie we've been taught about value being conditional. When you choose to make room for someone's full humanity, you are unlearning supremacy, capitalism, and shame in real time. Being a safe space doesn't mean avoiding discomfort.

It means staying present through it. It means standing with someone while they shake, doubt, or unearth truths that have been buried for generations. It means holding the line when the world would rather discard them for being "too much." You become a living contradiction to every space that ever made them feel disposable. And that's revolution.

One healed space can ripple through communities. One soul that feels seen can become a beacon of hope for others. You don't need power in the traditional sense, but you need presence.

You don't need perfection—you need willingness. When you let people breathe freely around you, you're not just offering peace, you're offering a possibility. The potential for safety, dignity, and liberation isn't just an idea. It can be felt, embodied, and lived right here, right now, with you.

CHAPTER 5:
Reclaiming Your Story & Building
Resilience Beyond the Damage

Eventually, you must stop letting your pain be the narrator of your hellish story. That doesn't mean ignoring what happened. It means choosing to be more than what hurt you, more than what broke you, and more than the worst things you've survived.

Survival often leads you to believe that pain is the main character. You start judging your worth based on how much you've endured. Over time, you forget that the story could be about something gentle, something free. You forget there's more to you than just endurance.

Here's the thing: damage leaves a mark, but it doesn't define the entire story. You're still the one holding the pen, and you get to decide what kind of story this will be from now on. Take responsibility, shut the doors, silence your phone, and get ready to do the difficult work that's needed.

Don't sugarcoat it; be honest with yourself. Reclaiming your story isn't easy. It's not about repeating affirmations or covering wounds with silver linings.

It involves carefully examining what happened, acknowledging it, feeling it, and taking responsibility for its impact without letting it control your actions. Resilience starts when you stop pretending you're okay, when you begin being honest about what hurts, and still choose to move forward. As with all things, never underestimate the power of choice; you can choose to move on or stay stuck in your delusion.

Healing isn't a straight path, so trust me when I say you'll revisit old pain. You'll have days when the story slips back into familiar language and patterns, and that's okay. Reclaiming doesn't mean you're going backward; it means refusing to be controlled by what has already happened and choosing action over autopilot, time and again.

There's a moment when you realize you've allowed someone else's voice to dominate your thoughts. It might be your parents, a bully, or a system that made you feel invisible. Whatever it is, it has influenced who you are, but it doesn't have to control your future.

These voices aren't just memories; they are inner critics. They constantly undermine your confidence, making you doubt yourself, play it safe, and stay silent. Reclaiming your story involves dismissing that critic and letting your voice drown out the echoes.

So, you begin exploring more deeply than ever before, asking yourself, "Is this belief even mine?" You notice when you shrink yourself in rooms where you should be standing tall. You pay attention to the stories you tell about who you are and what you deserve, then start rewriting them, line by line, not all at once— just the parts that no longer fit.

You might mourn those parts, even the painful ones, because they were familiar. They helped you survive, but clarity often comes at the expense of comfort. Growth involves leaving behind versions of yourself that once felt like home, even if they were shaped by fear.

It's not about pretending you have all the answers. Resilience isn't about being perfect. It's about showing up regardless, even when your hands are trembling.

It's facing fear while having the fear of failing. It's failing, and not accepting failure as your identity. It's falling and still getting back up because something within you refuses to quit.

The version of you that keeps showing up is your resilience in its purest form. It's not flashy, it's not perfect, but it is consistent. It's the quiet "try again" when everything in you wants to disappear. It's the whisper that says, "You're not done yet."

Whatever you haven't finished is that special *something* that makes it all worth it. That's the fire you protect. That's your source code. That's what no damage can take from you unless you choose to give it away.

Reclaiming your narrative involves telling the truth about where you've been without getting stuck there. It means saying, "Yes, that happened. But this is who I'm becoming." You stop auditioning for worthiness, stop explaining your existence, and stop shrinking to fit into rooms that were never built for your magic.

Now you can start creating a version of yourself rooted in your true essence, rather than in the person shaped by your need to survive. Since survival mode isn't permanent, eventually you'll stop avoiding pain. At some point, you'll want to welcome joy, love, peace, and possibility.

Transitioning can feel unsettling. When struggle has been your guiding compass, joy might seem uncertain. Peace can feel like a trap, but that's just your nervous system adjusting, so embrace it. You don't have to earn peace by first enduring suffering.

You're allowed to outgrow the struggle. You're allowed to thrive. You're allowed to write chapters that have nothing to do with trauma, proving people wrong, or carrying the weight of your past.

You're not obligated to keep carrying what broke you just because you learned how to hold it. You can set it down, not because it didn't matter, but because it doesn't have to define your next chapter. Here lies an opportunity to start fresh, not because the past didn't matter, but because you've finally realized you're more than that.

Yeah, your story began in chaos, loss, or rejection. Perhaps it's the result of a thousand silent wounds. But you're still here. You're still writing. And that means there's still time to create something beautiful. Something bold. Something that feels like *you.*

Maybe for the first time, you're not writing for approval or to be saved. You're writing because your voice deserves to be heard. Loud. Unapologetic. Unedited. That's not ego. That's liberation.

Don't let the damage define the whole story. Pick up the pen. Write forward.

Every time you speak your truth, you reclaim the space taken by silence. You're not just telling your story; you're rewriting the narrative that says you can't have one unless it's neat, polished, or pleasing. Forget that.

Your voice isn't just a performance. It's a weapon, a healing power, a declaration that says, *"I lived through hell, and I still get to speak."*

When the world tells you to tone it down, soften your edge, or be easier to digest, you write louder and messier. You express the parts they tried to erase as a form of catharsis, but in hell, that's rebellion. Because your words disrupt systems and challenge narratives that profit from your shame, they serve as a reminder that survival doesn't have to be quiet, that pain can fuel art, and that scars can symbolize a form of freedom.

Write as if the page is sacred because it is. Not because it's neat, but because it holds what the world tried to hide. You are not here to be small. You are here to make noise, shake cages, and show others that the pen is more than ink — it's a torch, and it's your light to lead the way.

CHAPTER 6: Community & Connection —Solutions to Isolation

Despite the false beliefs you've been taught in hell, we weren't meant to do this alone. I don't care how independent you are or how self-reliant you've become. You're still wired for connection.

You still need real people who see, hear, and don't flinch when you're falling apart. These connections may seem rare, even if you've reached out before and faced judgment or, worse, silence. Maybe you were vulnerable once, and someone took advantage of that.

Now you hesitate, convincing yourself you're better off alone. Even if part of you knows that's not true, that's how isolation begins—as a defense, not a choice. Once you peel back all the layers behind the isolation, you must admit that your comfort is confident cowardice.

The problem is that isolation can sometimes feel easier. Safer. Quieter. You tell yourself you're protecting your peace, but often you're just trying not to bleed on people who won't know how to handle your pain.

So, you go silent. You ghost everyone. You build a life based on avoidance and call it boundaries. However, this is where it gets tricky, because isolation can sometimes seem like a form of healing.

You decline plans, stop replying to messages, and convince yourself that solitude equals growth. But actual boundaries create space for connection, while isolation builds walls. One protects you, and the other hides you.

For a while, that might have worked to some degree because keeping your distance kept you sane. But here's the truth no one wants to admit aloud: isolation is a slow form of death. It tricks you into thinking you're okay when, in fact, you're just numb. It convinces you that disconnection means strength when it's grief in disguise.

It becomes a quiet kind of grief that never fully reveals itself. You start to forget what it's like to laugh without censoring yourself, to cry in front of someone without feeling like a burden. The pain of not being seen becomes your new normal, and you begin to settle into the loneliness as if it's your home.

Healing requires ethical and moral witnesses. It needs mirrors. It needs someone to look at you and say, "You're not crazy. I've felt that too." You don't always need advice; you need presence.

You need someone who won't try to fix you because they understand that just being with you is enough. If you've never experienced that, I get it. It's hard to trust what you've never seen, but that doesn't make it any less important.

If anything, it makes this need even more crucial. The longer you go without a safe connection, the more unfamiliar it feels. And the more unfamiliar it seems, the easier it is to reject. This creates a cycle: craving closeness, fearing it, pushing it away, and then wondering why you still feel so lonely.

There's a reason loneliness hurts so deeply. It's not only emotional; it's biological. Your body sees disconnection as a threat, and your nervous system reacts strongly.

You don't sleep well. You don't eat well. You either over-express or completely shut down. In that state, everything becomes distorted. You start to believe the lie that you're too much, too broken, or too far gone to be loved.

Isolation deceives you, as it distorts your reflection. You start to see yourself through the lens of absence, as a burden, as an afterthought, as someone who doesn't belong anywhere. Belonging isn't something you earn by being perfect—it's something you remember by being honest with yourself.

But the truth is this: you're not perfect—you never were. You just needed the right kind of space that doesn't shame your process. A space where people make room for your humanity instead of demanding that you perform wellness you haven't earned yet.

That kind of connection addresses unresolved issues that therapy might not resolve. It's not because treatment isn't effective, but because belonging resonates differently. Belonging communicates to your nervous system, "You're safe now." It rewires you and restores what isolation has distorted.

It doesn't even have to be a deep conversation. Sometimes, just sitting silently next to someone without feeling the need to perform or explain is enough. It's that quiet recalibration of your nervous system — the exhale that says, "Okay. I'm safe here."

And no, a "safe space" isn't always easy to find. Sometimes, you have to build it from the ground up. Sometimes, you need to be the one who reaches out first, even when your pride is telling you to stay quiet. Sometimes, you have to risk being awkward, rejected, and vulnerable to find someone who truly understands you.

Yes, it's risky, but vulnerability always is, and you will make mistakes a few times. You might reach out to the wrong people, but every effort is a step out of the darkness. Every moment you allow yourself to be seen, even just a little, is part of the unlearning process. You're practicing connection, even when it feels unstable.

But it's worth it because healing within the community grows each time. When you share your truth, someone else shares theirs, and something sacred happens. Something sacred that says, "You don't have to carry this alone anymore."

If you've been trying to heal in hell, surrounded by people who invalidate you, environments that drain you, or silence that slowly suffocates you, make it easy to feel stuck. Hell is loud with judgment and quiet with empathy. No one heals when they're constantly bracing for harm.

Healing isn't about always being hypervigilant. It's about finally relaxing your shoulders, speaking your truth without fear of consequences, crying without apology, and laughing without shrinking away. A secure connection enables you to lower your defenses, allowing you to rest without fear.

Perhaps the real shift isn't about doing more inner work or reading another self-help book. Maybe it's about opening up to someone, saying, "This is where I'm at," and allowing connection to achieve what isolation never could. In this shared space of vulnerability, we find the empathy and support needed to heal in ways we can't do alone.

It's easy to idolize independence when society teaches you that needing others is a weakness. However, this is a lie. It's just another story created by systems like capitalism and colonialism that rely on isolation. True strength is not found in standing alone, but in the courage to build and rely on a network of reciprocal support.

Do you realize the system is selling you rugged individualism so you don't see how powerful we are when we unite? Because if we link arms, listen, lift, and love each other through the chaos, they can't divide us, exploit us, or profit from our isolation. Our interdependence isn't a vulnerability to be exploited but a revolutionary force capable of building a more open-minded and loving world.

Letting someone in isn't just a personal act; in today's world, it's political. It challenges the idea that silence equals strength and opposes the notion that vulnerability indicates weakness. When you share your pain, grief, joy, and chaos with someone, you participate in a mutual form of liberation. You're saying, *I trust you to hold part of this with me,* and *I'm no longer ashamed of being human.*

Letting someone in isn't a sign of weakness; it's a sign of intelligence and survival. It's saying, "I'm done trying to carry this weight alone." Because some burdens were never meant to be carried solo, some wounds only close when witnessed, and some stories only make sense when spoken out loud.

We weren't meant to heal alone. We are meant to heal in circles, through songs and stories. Again, we weren't meant to heal alone. Instead, we're meant to heal in circles, through songs, stories, shared meals, long pauses, and deep listening.

The revolution isn't always televised. Sometimes, it appears as two people in a quiet room sharing the truth for the first time. Sometimes, it begins there and spreads like wildfire.

You don't have to be perfect to be loved. You don't have to be healed to belong. You need to be willing to come out of hiding.

Is it because you believe you must be whole before you're worthy? If so, understand that this is manipulative mind control. That's how systems keep you silent by making you think your brokenness disqualifies you from community, from love, or from being seen.

Your completeness isn't a requirement for worthiness. It's the result of being embraced while still being incomplete, if you will. The revolution begins when you stop waiting to be perfect and start showing up as you are.

Stepping out of hiding is a brave act of defiance in a world that punishes vulnerability and exploits suffering. When you say, "Here I am—flawed, open, and still healing," you are rejecting shame as a weapon. You are reclaiming visibility from a society that prefers your pain to stay hidden behind closed doors. You are standing in your truth, not because it's polished, but because it's yours, and that in itself is sacred.

This is how we change culture, not by presenting curated versions of ourselves, but by building relationships that can embrace our mess. Radical love doesn't require you to be perfect. It simply asks you to be honest. You don't become worthy by healing; healing helps you remember that you were always worthy from the moment of your birth.

CHAPTER 7:
Self-Care as Resistance &
Prioritizing Your Well-Being

You know what no one tells you? Choosing yourself can sometimes upset people, and why wouldn't they be upset? Especially if they are unaware of the hell inside them and the environment that created it.

It might disappoint, confuse, or even make them question who you are. But don't fight it because you need to go through it. You have to choose for yourself, regardless.

As difficult as it may be, making a choice can initially bring loneliness. It is the silence that follows when you say no. It is the distance that grows when you stop bending over backward.

But that space is where your peace will find you. It's where you will meet yourself without all the noise. Because if you don't, no one else will do it for you, and that's what *self-care* is all about.

It's not always about a spa day, lighting candles, and journaling your feelings in perfect handwriting. Sometimes it's messy. Sometimes it's saying no and truly meaning it. Sometimes it's severing ties you believed were permanent. Sometimes it's eating, sleeping, and resting while the world around you is screaming, "Keep grinding."

Self-care can often seem like rebellion when you've spent your entire life equating busyness with worth, when rest feels like failure, and when stillness brings guilt. But proper self-care requires you to unlearn that noise. It asks you to stop judging your value by how much you can endure before breaking.

We live in a culture that profits from your burnout and romanticizes exhaustion. It tells you that your worth is tied to your productivity, appearance, and performance. You see, when you start opting out of that and decide that your peace matters more than your image, that's resistance.

Resistance doesn't always roar; sometimes it looks like staying home instead of being someone else's emotional crutch. Sometimes it means leaving a group chat, canceling a dinner, and choosing solitude over performance. That quiet defiance? That's where your healing starts.

Taking care of yourself in a world that benefits from your self-neglect—that's a radical act. That's not indulgence. That's survival. That's strategy. That's you refusing to let the chaos of hell swallow you whole.

Believe me, I get it. Putting yourself first might feel foreign, especially if you were raised to be the one who fixes everything. The strong one. The reliable one. The one who ensures everyone else is taken care of before considering their own needs.

You probably learned early that self-abandonment was the price of being loved, or that being "easy" and "low-maintenance" kept you safe. But safety isn't the same as being whole. At some point, you have to stop bleeding for people who wouldn't even hand you a bandage. Stop proving your worth by silently enduring pain.

In a hellish world, we forget that we are not here to serve as everyone else's landing pad while we fall through the floor. If the love you receive requires your silence, exhaustion, or invisibility, then it's not love. So please understand that it's okay to walk away when compassion is no longer offered.

Taking care of yourself isn't selfish; it makes you sustainable. It prevents you from becoming resentful and empty. It's more than just bubble baths or digital detoxes. It's about making daily choices that proclaim, "I matter."

Embracing this kind of decision-making changes everything. It involves choosing meals that nourish rather than numb you, and answering calls based on preference instead of feeling obligated to pick up every call. You learn that you have to let others down if it means staying loyal to your values, because that's what self-respect looks like in practice.

If you're looking for actions that speak louder than words, your search ends here. Let your boundaries be respected, and recognize when to say, "I don't have the capacity for this conversation right now." It's about removing yourself from those who drain your energy and not feeling guilty about it. It's also about listening to your body and giving it what it needs, rather than punishing it for not performing as you think it should.

Your body isn't a machine, but it sends us a clear message. When it aches, shuts down, or feels heavy, it's not betraying you; it's trying to tell you something. Ask it what it needs, not what it can produce. Healing begins when you stop fighting against your biology.

Sometimes, self-care can be boring. Whether it's doing your laundry, logging off your device, or going to therapy when you'd rather cancel, it's about facing your patterns instead of blaming everyone else. It's not always soft or pretty, but it's always powerful.

The truth is that no one is coming to save you, and no one will give you permission to rest. You must save yourself and choose to grant yourself permission, because your well-being isn't up for negotiation. Others might not understand, but remember that being misunderstood is part of the journey to escape hell.

It doesn't matter what anyone believes. Protecting yourself and allowing yourself to do so is non-negotiable. Because it's non-negotiable, be okay with being misunderstood. Let "them" gossip, question, call you selfish, or dramatic.

You're no longer living for their comfort. You're creating a life that doesn't demand sacrificing your sanity to maintain peace. Such a sacrifice is insanity, pure and simple.

So if you're waiting for the world to slow down and make room for your healing, you'll be waiting forever. You have to create that space. You have to carve it out, protect it, and fight for it if necessary.

Because your holistic health, whether it's mental, physical, or emotional, is not a luxury. It's the foundation of all aspects of your life and influences every step you take. Without making space to heal and being in a position to heal when needed, nothing else can stand.

So no, you're not being dramatic. You're not asking for too much. You're not lazy for needing rest. You're done being available to things that keep you unwell, and that is the most honest and powerful form of self-care there is.

Every time you say no to what drains you, you say *"yes"* to what restores you. If you think otherwise, then now is the time to learn the difference between what is selfish and what is sacred. Protecting your peace safeguards your purpose, because you can't pour from a cracked cup.

Prioritize yourself. Not because you're more important than anyone else, but because you've finally realized you're not less. This shift isn't an act of selfishness but a radical act of self-worth and self-love that allows you to show up more fully for both yourself and others, and in hell, that's not the norm. Those around you will notice and may be spiteful that you've made that change for your well-being.

Choosing yourself in a world that profits from your self-neglect is an act of rebellion. The system is designed to keep you exhausted, compliant, stretched thin, and questioning your worth, because a burnt-out person doesn't resist; the rest is resistance. Boundaries are a form of defiance. Every time you say, "I matter enough to stop here," you are rejecting the grind culture that seeks to turn your life into a transaction.

Reclamation has nothing to do with ego. You're reclaiming your time, energy, voice, and body from every structure, system, and relationship that tried to convince you that your value was based on how useful, agreeable, or invisible you could be. But you are anything but that, and it's time you align with who you are.

You weren't born to be consumed. You were born to create, to thrive, to choose joy without explanation. You were born to pursue your dreams, your vision, and your piece of heaven on Earth.

So protect your peace as if it were a protest, because it is. Your wellness challenges a world that profits from your suffering. Your healing shatters the foundation of every lie that said you had to earn your right to be okay. You don't, and guess what, you never did.

CHAPTER 8:
Rituals for Healing, Liberation, and Growth

Healing isn't always loud, but hell would lead one to believe it has to be. Sometimes it's the smallest thing, like drinking water first thing in the morning instead of scrolling or taking three deep breaths before reacting. Maybe it's saying, "I need space," instead of exploding, and deciding that escaping the hell inside of you is more important than living in it another day.

These actions might not always seem like rituals, but they are. They are the actions you take to reassure your nervous system that you're safe, no longer in survival mode, and free to feel something other than panic. In this *intentional repetition*, you are actively reprogramming your body to embrace peace and regulate itself in the present moment.

Physiologically, your body doesn't always believe you at first, and to be honest, why would it? Let's say you attempt to do the ritual, and maybe it doesn't work right away. Maybe your chest still tightens, and that's okay. Accept the process for what it is, and know that's not failure; it's recalibration.

Healing rituals are about consistency, not perfection. They're a way of teaching your system that safety isn't a fluke, it's a "new normal." Surprisingly, even this new normal presents itself as one of the most challenging barriers to our healing.

For a long time, I thought healing had to be this big, dramatic breakthrough. A retreat of some sort, like a motion picture film production of a personal psycho-emotional purge, complete with a full soundtrack and incense burning in the background. In some ways, I can see how one could be led to believe such a thing.

But in reality, it's quiet, personal, and awkward. But as long as you know that it's you trying something different, even though it feels unnatural, you'll be fine. Because truthfully? Freedom feels weird at first when you've been living in *a cage.*

You'll second-guess it, sabotage it, and miss the comfort of your dysfunction, because at least it was familiar. But follow the necessary steps, because that's what happens when you start growing out of your trauma identity. You've lived in a hellish world, where living a hellish life of normalized trauma will do that to you.

Freedom doesn't feel like freedom right away. Usually, it feels like exposure, like vulnerability—and as many of you know, vulnerability isn't always a strong suit in a hellish world. It's the raw edge of becoming someone you haven't fully met yet.

Rituals matter because they reconnect you with yourself. They break through the chaos. They signal the transition from who you were to who you're becoming.

You don't need anyone else's permission to create them. You don't need a guru, a manual, or a TikTok aesthetic. You need *intention.* You need *presence.*

Ritual is more about why you do it than *what* you do. It's how you remind yourself, "I deserve care." It's how you pause the world's demands long enough to remember your own needs. It's not about adding more to your to-do list — it's about removing what's been draining your energy without asking.

Light a candle if it helps, or don't. Sit silently in your car for five minutes before heading inside. Cry in the shower. Write letters you never sent, or dance around your kitchen in your oldest hoodie, because that's healing too.

Let's be unapologetically clear: Healing doesn't have to be dramatic to be real. Sometimes, the most powerful rituals are the ones that appear ordinary, such as brushing your teeth after a depressive episode, saying no without justifying it, or sitting with a feeling instead of running from it. Those quiet, consistent acts? They add up.

I think we have to be reminded of that, some more than others, because we forget that growth isn't always graceful. Sometimes your rituals involve setting alarms to remind you to eat. Sometimes they're about deleting numbers and blocking the source of the chaos. Not because you hate them, but because you love yourself enough to stop reopening wounds and calling it loyalty.

We don't talk enough about how often healing means prioritizing yourself in ways that may seem selfish to others. Especially when the people around you have gotten used to the version of you that always says yes, that always stays quiet, that always puts them first. But liberation means disappointing people who benefited from your self-neglect.

You can create your own moments of peace. You don't have to wait for your environment to change. Hell might still be around you, but healing is what you carve out inside of that.

Despite living in a modern world, we forget that liberation is not a destination. It's something you create, like eating an elephant—you do it bite by bite. We should build ourselves the same way: brick by brick, breath by breath, and choice by choice.

Some days, that choice feels small, insignificant, and like you're just going through the motions. Over time, those tiny choices start to layer, creating a rhythm and pattern—a new story. Soon, the ground beneath you begins to feel different—more solid, more like your own.

Your rituals don't need to make sense to anyone else. They don't have to look pretty. They need to be yours.

Do you make coffee or tea and journal for ten minutes each morning? If that's your daily routine, that's great. Do you scream or sing in your car on your way home from work? If that's part of your routine, then that's also great.

Do you light something, burn something, plant something, or breathe through something? All of it counts. All of it moves the needle, even if no one else sees it.

Because healing isn't meant for the highlight reel, it's not always something to share. Some of your deepest work will happen in silence, in solitude, with no one clapping for you, and still, it counts. Still, it matters. Some of your most life-changing growth will go unnoticed by the world, but your soul will feel it deeply.

Healing isn't always heroic. It often means coming back to yourself again and again. It's better to accept the chaos than wait to feel perfect before starting. *Spoiler alert: You don't have to be perfect to begin; you need to be willing.*

Willingness doesn't mean you know exactly what to do. It means you're open to trying new things. It means you're tired of carrying the same pain, and you're curious about what else is possible.

You don't need a plan. You need to say yes to starting, even if it's messy or slow. As I mentioned before, healing isn't about perfection; it's about consistency—taking that first step makes a big difference.

Want growth? Stop waiting for it to be convenient and start honoring the rituals that bring you back to life, whatever they may be or how they appear.

If you fall off track? That's not a sign to give up. It's a reminder to get back on course.

Your healing rituals aren't about perfection; they're about returning again and again. I keep saying it's sacred because that's the part many people seem to struggle with understanding. Not that you never fall, but that you keep coming back to yourself, and yourself is all you've got. Regardless of who else claims they have your best interests at heart.

If you don't realize it by now, acknowledge that you deserve to feel free now. Not someday, not when it's perfect—Now. And if no one has told you yet, you're doing better than you think, because *this* is the start.

Every time you return to yourself, after the spiral, after the silence, after the slip, you're refusing the narrative that says you have to be flawless to be whole. That is revolution. The "world" wants your healing to be linear, clean, and easy to digest.

To escape the burning embers and the flames of fiery psycho-emotional traumas and unresolved pain that we've compartmentalized in hell, we have to accept that real healing is gritty, nonlinear, and deeply personal. Coming back to yourself in the middle of the mess is a radical declaration that you are still worthy, still sacred, and still yours. No matter what, embrace this discomfort during the healing process, as it is necessary for escape.

This is how systems begin to lose power over you—not when you hit some final stage of enlightenment, but when you stop *outsourcing your worth.* When your rituals become your resistance, whether you light the candle, take the breath, say the prayer, or scream into the pillow, not for show, but because you know peace isn't something you wait for. It's something you claim, again and again, for yourself—unapologetically.

Your healing doesn't need an audience; it only requires your permission to be vulnerable, to be slow, and to be real. You are not broken for needing to begin again; you are powerful because you do. And it is your choice to remain broken and lost in hell.

CHAPTER 9:
Transforming Pain into Power: Movement from Surviving to Thriving

Hell is filled with pain, and pain changes you. Let's start there. Sometimes pain doesn't even come with a warning. It arrives disguised as burnout, as a slow unraveling, as silence where there once was connection.

Not all pain is loud or obvious. Some of it settles in quietly, convincing you that this is just how life is now. That heaviness? It's not a personality trait; it's grief with nowhere to go.

It doesn't ask for permission or wait for a good time. It just shows up, crashes in, wrecks everything, and challenges you to figure out how to live afterward, and survive? That's what you do when you're still bleeding but life keeps demanding your attention.

But in hell, the culture of dysfunction requires you to figure out how to keep moving forward, even when nothing makes sense. Even when you're numb, tired, angry, or all three at once. Hell's system depends on your overall dysfunction and benefits from you being stuck in a hellish state, which is precisely where you need to be—in hell.

But in hell, that culture of dysfunction is entirely about survival. Survival shouldn't be the ultimate goal, and it isn't. It's just the hallway point. It's where you catch your breath, patch yourself up, and try to remember who you were before the chaos, or maybe meet who you're becoming now.

Thriving, though? That's a whole different thing. Thriving is what happens when you stop trying to prove you deserve to be here, when you stop bracing for the next hit, and when you stop defining yourself by the damage and start building something with it, not despite it.

The shift doesn't happen all at once; it creeps in. Quietly. Usually, after a hundred moments when you could have collapsed but didn't.

Transforming pain into power isn't about pretending it didn't hurt. It's not about smiling through it or turning it into some inspirational Instagram caption. It's about facing it, allowing it to be ugly, and letting it teach you without letting it control you.

There is value in rage. There is wisdom in sorrow. Your emotions are messengers, not enemies. We've been conditioned to ignore our feelings and to "stay strong," to "rise above it."

But what if facing your pain and letting it show is really what makes a difference? Sometimes, you need to scream into a pillow or break down in the shower before anything can be healed. Sometimes you have to be broken down before you can be built up again.

It's about asking, "What now?" Not, "Why me?" Not, "What if?," but "What now?" "What do I do with what I've seen, what I've survived, and what I've learned the hard way?" If you've never asked yourself these questions, then now *is* the time.

You begin to notice where the pain has cracked something open, rather than simply breaking it down. You also start to see the moments that used to trigger you, whether they are conversations, specific spaces, or particular dynamics. You realize they no longer affect you the same way. Welcome to growth.

The shift is subtle but genuine. You realize you're no longer reacting from the same wounds. You might still feel the sting, but you don't fall apart. That is the muscle memory of resilience forming in real time.

You start to realize that some of your strength was born in the middle of the wreckage. You discover what you're truly made of, not because someone told you, but because you survived something that could have broken your spirit. Somehow, you're still here, and yes, you may be scarred. You may be limping, but *here you are*.

Thriving isn't some perfect healed version of you skipping through life with no baggage. Thriving means you've made peace with the fact that the pain changed you, and you still chose to grow anyway. You still chose joy where bitterness could've lived. You still chose love where trust had been shattered. You still showed up.

The shift from just surviving to truly thriving can be subtle, as it involves saying yes to new opportunities without over-explaining. It's about choosing rest over hustle when your worth isn't on the line. It means speaking up for yourself without spiraling out of control afterward. It's that moment when you genuinely laugh and realize you weren't just pretending.

Sometimes, thriving is about reclaiming the parts of yourself that got buried under trauma. Your creativity. Your voice. Your softness. Your dreams. You don't owe anyone a version of yourself that's easier to handle. You get to be all of it. Loud, quiet, tender, wild. Whole.

Pain will shape you, but you hold the power to decide what it creates. So no, this chapter of your life doesn't have to be about barely hanging on. It can be about becoming. About rising. About transforming the parts of you that hurt the most into the parts that hold the most extraordinary wisdom.

You're no longer just surviving. You're creating something. You're becoming someone.

You're planting seeds. Some won't bloom immediately. Some might surprise you with what they develop into.

But you're moving forward. You're shaping a future where your power isn't just a reaction to pain. It's a commitment to possibility, and that's not just brave, it's revolutionary.

Maybe it's time to stop doubting your worthiness for the next chapter and start writing it confidently. Write as if the page owes you, because it does. You've endured enough pain; now it's time to enjoy the rewards of your liberation.

Because worthiness was never the question; that was the lie, planted by systems that feared what you might become if you stopped doubting yourself, stopped shrinking yourself, and stopped waiting for permission to rise. Your next chapter doesn't require perfection; it requires *audacity*. It requires the courage to imagine more, to demand better, and to build what you were told you didn't deserve.

This isn't about healing quietly in the corner. It's about rebuilding the entire foundation. Your story isn't just personal—it's political. Every time you choose joy over guilt, rest over grind, and truth over silence, you're breaking generational curses and redefining what power looks like.

I cannot stress this enough: *speaking out about healing is a threat to every system that relies on your silence.* When you center your joy, your rest, your humanity, you're refusing to be complicit in your erasure. You're not just rewriting your story; you're burning down the narratives that kept you small, obedient, and grateful for crumbs.

That's not just easy work. That's defiance. That's you realizing you're a rebel with more than a cause—*this is a movement.*

Don't let anyone tell you that it's too much, that you're too loud, or that you're too radical. This has been said about every movement that has ever created change. Don't trick yourself into doubting, shrinking, or asking for permission from this point on.

Honoring your wholeness in a world that profits from your fragmentation is about resistance—ethical and moral resistance. Don't let anything stop you from having your own revolution in real time. Don't allow anyone to whisper anything that makes you question your decision, because you're not just healing; you're shaking things up.

So, take up space, go at your own pace, and grab the damn mic. The foundation was never built to support you. For once, do what you've probably wanted to do for a long time: build your own. Create a foundation that is fearlessly rooted in truth, power, and liberation, and watch what emerges.

CHAPTER 10:
Building Your Sanctuary:
Maintaining Long-Term Mental Wellness

You can't keep healing in chaos and expect it to last. You can do all the inner work, read every book, and cry through all the breakthroughs you can imagine. However, if you continue to return to places and spaces that drain you, interact with people who don't respect your boundaries, and engage in routines that tire your body, the healing won't take root. It'll feel like trying to dry off while standing in the rain.

The point is, most of us don't notice we're soaked until we stop for a moment and realize how cold we've become. We accept the rain as usual. We tell ourselves it's just part of life, just part of growing up, just how it is.

But just because you're used to something doesn't mean it's not hurting you. Familiar isn't the same as healthy. Surviving isn't the same as truly living.

This is where the idea of a sanctuary comes into play. No, I don't mean a perfect little Zen room filled with crystals and essential oils, unless that's your thing. I mean something intense, impactful, and built for long-lasting sustainability.

You need a sanctuary that offers a life where you feel safe to live, a mind that feels like a place you don't want to leave, and a nervous system that isn't constantly on high alert. This is a reality that intentionally makes space for your peace. Such a sanctuary isn't a reward or luxury—it's a necessity.

If you've spent years in survival mode, peace might seem suspicious. Too quiet. Too still.

You might sabotage it or start fights to feel something familiar. Here's the fine line between failure and conditioning, so it takes time to trust peace again. To believe that ease isn't a trap, and that calm isn't just the quiet before the next storm.

Because the truth is, mental wellness doesn't come from constant hustle. It doesn't come from always being busy, always pushing through, or always acting like you're fine when you're unraveling inside. Long-term peace comes from *structure*, through choice. *Honor what keeps you grounded instead of what distracts you.*

Ask yourself: What truly nourishes you? What activities leave you feeling clearer, calmer, and fulfilled, and what numbs you out? There's a difference between rest and escape, between recovery and avoidance. Building a sanctuary means understanding this difference and choosing what restores your spirit, even if it's not the easiest or most popular option.

You start building your sanctuary when you stop waiting for someone else to give you permission to feel good. It's established when you stop making excuses for chaos just because it's familiar. When you realize your healing can't depend on someone else changing first.

If someone else caused your pain, it's a tough truth to face. It's easy to wait for an apology, closure, or justice. But waiting too long can become its own kind of prison. Sometimes, reclaiming your peace means choosing yourself, even if no one else shows up the way you needed them to.

It's in the routines you hold dear. It's how you unwind at night behind closed doors. It's what you say to yourself in the mirror.

Whether you let your phone control your mornings or give others access to your energy at any time, those people, places, or things either refill your cup or drain it until it's empty. The truth is in how you talk to yourself when no one's listening. Self-empowerment depends on how you center yourself when life tries to pull you off balance.

Your sanctuary isn't just a physical space; it's also an emotional and mental one. It's how you respond when chaos hits. Is your first instinct to panic, go numb, or spiral? Or, can you reach for something grounding?

Grounding can be as simple as a breath, a phrase, or a ritual. As long as it reminds you, "I've been here before. I know what to do." That's sanctuary in motion.

It's not about being "disciplined" 24/7. It's about being devoted—devoted to your peace, clarity, and wellness. But don't be gullible; you can't rely on hope alone for wellness.

You must intentionally build a life that maintains hope by avoiding the romanticizing of dysfunction. This means not confusing survival mode with true strength. It also involves recognizing when your mind is urging you to slow down and paying close attention to your thoughts.

The goal isn't to create a stress-free life because that's not realistic. Life will continue, people will disappoint you, and things will fall apart.

However, a sanctuary creates a space in your life that is designed for ease, rest, and reconnecting with yourself. Essentially, you're less likely to be knocked down easily and recover more quickly. You trust yourself more and stop abandoning yourself when things get tough.

It's not just about healing; it's about maintaining that healing. It's about creating rhythms that support you, rituals that soothe you, and boundaries that protect you when you're not feeling strong. The truth is that true well-being is an ongoing practice of self-regulation and careful self-care, not a one-time goal.

You don't have to earn rest. You don't need to reach burnout to justify taking a step back. You have the right to prioritize your wellness before everything falls apart, and if that idea feels selfish or unfamiliar, that's likely the work you need to focus on right away.

Rest is a right, not a reward earned through burnout. But many of us are taught the opposite, that worth is based on endurance and that exhaustion is a badge of honor. As a result, rest often feels unnatural.

Living in "hell" actually requires you to start healing and unlearning the identity linked to the grind. For too long, we've had it backwards, believing that "the grind" is the key to healing. We are intentionally programmed to think that external success will boost our internal worth.

However, external achievements only provide a temporary measure of your true worth. People who depend on this often learn the hard way and face serious consequences. This mindset doesn't automatically lead to inner enlightenment, but it highlights the importance of being present instead of just doing, and valuing results over performance.

So ask yourself, "What do I need more of to feel steady?" "What do I need less of?" "Who in my life causes chaos?" "Who brings peace?" "What small change could make my space feel more like a soft landing and less like a battleground?"

Sanctuary doesn't always mean escaping to a distant place. Sometimes, it simply means lowering the volume, choosing stillness, and making peace your baseline rather than just your recovery plan. And to even do this, you have to make the bold decision of choosing yourself above all else.

This may involve disappointing others, but it's worth it. It might mean missing out on things that drain you, avoiding conversations that trigger you, or saying "no" when you've been conditioned to say "yes." But every time you choose peace over performance, you strengthen your sanctuary. You make the courageous decision to center yourself, and that's a sacred, not a selfish act.

No one ever told you *"you're allowed to feel good,"* and not just in short bursts. Not just when you've earned it; you can feel that way all the time. That's not too much to ask, and that's the whole point.

You were never meant to survive on scraps of joy. This system wants you to believe that feeling good is a luxury, a prize you earn after exhaustion, productivity, or self-erasure. But that's a lie built to keep you small, compliant, and chronically reaching for approval.

The truth? Feeling good, and I mean that deep, sustained, unapologetic good, is your birthright. Not a reward. It is the complete and total baseline of life.

Imagine the possibilities when pleasure, peace, and rest are normalized rather than rationed. When you stop bracing for disappointment, life becomes easier each time. When joy isn't just a fleeting guest, but your default setting, that isn't indulgence; it's liberation, and it's terrifying to a world built on your suffering.

So stop apologizing for wanting ease. Stop shrinking around your delight. Your wellness doesn't need to be justified.

You don't need to prove your pain to earn your peace. You are allowed to feel good simply because you exist. There is no better time than the present moment to stop asking for permission; that's when the revolution begins.

CONCLUSION:
This Is Not The End

Let's clarify: this isn't where the story ends. You've read every page, faced every truth, and held tightly to your pain. But this isn't closure—it's a spark.

You didn't come all this way to feel inspired for five minutes and then return to your cage. You didn't dig this deep to decorate the walls of your prison with pretty affirmations. No.

You came *here* to wake the hell up—to remember that healing was never meant to be soft, sterile, or palatable to power. Healing, in a place like this, is insurrection. It's rebellion. It's your soul ripping the gag off its mouth and saying, "I am not here to behave."

Every time you reclaim your time, rest, joy, rage, softness, and story, you're challenging a system built to reduce you to just a function, not a human. They want you silent, obedient, and always broken. They prefer your therapy to be performative, your recovery rushed, your voice a whisper, and your pain something they can sell.

But you know better now.

You know that unlearning is just as sacred as learning. That quitting what harms you is just as powerful as pushing through. That leaving systems, relationships, and mindsets that suffocate your spirit is not weakness—it's warriorship.

You have no obligation to make yourself digestible. No duty to sit quietly at tables that were never built for you. This time, you're building your own. Brick by brick. Story by story. Breath by breath.

Please know that this foundation won't be built on self-abandonment. It won't be built on shame. It won't be built on trauma dressed up as tradition.

This foundation is radical, it's disruptive, and it's yours. Your healing is not up for debate. Your liberation is not a negotiation. Your worth is not conditional.

So let's stop entertaining the bullshit ideas of what it means to be "resilient" in a world that eats people alive and calls it character building. Let's stop acting like survival is a personality trait and hypervigilance is a skillset. Let's stop calling it growth when all we're doing is suffering more efficiently.

This is your line in the sand. This is where you stop internalizing the chaos and start externalizing your power. This is where you stop being impressed by performance and start honoring your peace. This is where you stop asking for permission to heal and start protecting your right to exist fully.

Understand this: your healing is a delicate and potentially dangerous process. It is inconvenient to those who thrive off your disconnection. It is threatening to systems that count on you never questioning your pain. But do it anyway.

Heal loudly. Speak the truth. Take up space.

No more shrinkage. No more apologies. No more pretending, and if the world can't handle your wholeness, then let it break.

Because we're not rebuilding our lives just to fit into the old mold, we're not rising from the ashes to politely return to our cubicles of compliance. We are not surviving to maintain the status quo. We are becoming architects of new worlds—starting with the terrain inside our bodies.

Let the revolution begin there. Breathe like it's a protest. Rest like it's a demand. Cry like it's a spell. Laugh like it's resistance. Love like it's a revolution.

This is not just a book. This is your battle cry.

You know what hell feels like. Now it's time to embody what heaven on Earth might mean—on your terms, in your skin, through your walk, in your sound. You're not here to be saved. You're here to save yourself.

So, burn the map they gave you. It will only lead you back to where you started. And do you want to go back to complex trauma, neglect, abuse, and overwhelming negative self-talk?

Be the fire that keeps *you* warm. Do not be the one who burns alive trying to light up someone else's path. Be the heat that fuels *your healing*.

Be the flame that refuses to go out, even when the world keeps throwing water. Burn with purpose. Burn with truth. Let your light be a signal to every part of you that has ever felt lost in the dark: *you are your spark.*

For the first time, walk like you're finally free. This is not the end. This is the uprising.

Start HEALING—and ESCAPE THE HELL INSIDE OF YOU.

Shots fired. *Now, move...*

www.ingramcontent.com/pod-product-compliance
Lightning Source LLC
Chambersburg PA
CBHW071236290326
41931CB00038B/3208